RAND

Joint Warfighting Capabilities (JWCA) Integration

Report on Phase 1 Research

Leslie Lewis, John Schrader, William L. Schwabe, Roger A. Brown

Prepared for the
Joint Staff

National Defense Research Institute

Preface

This report documents Phase 1 of a RAND project to develop an analytic capability to assist the Joint Staff Requirements, Assessment, and Integration Division (RAID) in the J-8 Directorate in integrating the activities of Joint Warfighting Capabilities Assessment (JWCA) teams and the Joint Requirements Oversight Council (JROC). The goal of the study was to assist RAID in the identification of broad issues and their assessment utilizing the analytic architecture defined by RAND in previous J-8 work. Phase 1 required the application of the analytic framework to near-, mid-, and long-term resource issues. The inputs to the process were the various products of the JROC/JWCA process. The research team then applied the framework to several JWCA areas to demonstrate how broad issues might be defined and, through the further application of the framework, how they might be addressed in more detail. The process is described in this draft report. Subsequent phases will further refine the process in the identification and assessment of relevant joint issues.

The report should be of interest to policymakers and students concerned with the development and application of a discipline for defense resource decisionmaking—particularly a framework for strategy-to-tasks resource management.

This work was performed within the International Security and Defense Policy Center of RAND's National Defense Research Institute (NDRI), a federally funded research and development center sponsored by the Office of the Secretary of Defense, the Joint Staff, and the defense agencies. Comments should be directed to the authors or to Dr. Gregory Treverton, director of the International Security and Defense Policy Center.

Contents

Figures

Table

Summary

Background and Objectives

The 1986 Goldwater-Nichols legislation charged the Chairman of the Joint Chiefs of Staff (CJCS) with integrating strategic requirements and the requirements of the commanders in chief (CINCs) of the unified and specified commands. This responsibility placed an additional analytic burden on the Joint Staff, and RAND was asked to assist in identifying an overarching architecture that would help the Joint Staff define strategic and operational issues and their associated resource implications. In response, RAND developed a framework called Objectives-Based Resource Management (OBRM). This framework provides a way to analyze issues within a structure that links resources to national objectives. This framework assists the CJCS in prioritizing CINC requirements based on the national security strategy and in assessing the capabilities of the services and other organizations to meet CINC needs.

The JROC is the mechanism that identifies joint operational needs, reviews service proposals for meeting them, and approves requirements for materiel solutions. The JWCA process was created to assist the JROC in the integration of issues and assessment of capabilities that cut across services and functional areas. The JWCA teams are organized into ten joint functional areas for assessment. An organization in J-8, RAID, was charged with facilitating the integration activities of the JROC and JWCA.

The purpose of this project is to assist RAID in its integration efforts by applying the OBRM methodology. Its three objectives are to

- Identify some gaps or overlaps in the JWCA assessment areas and link them to the initiatives identified thus far
- Assist RAID in identifying a broad set of analytic tools to support the Joint Staff's analysis of the JWCA areas
- Assist RAID in integrating JWCA efforts.

JWCA and OBRM

The JWCA process was designed to focus on joint warfighting capabilities and to cover the spectrum of warfighting activities now and in the mid- and long terms.

This design ensures that any issues that arise can be assigned to a JWCA area. The goal was to assist the senior defense leadership in making informed choices in an era of constrained budgets. The process identifies constraints that hinder the Department of Defense (DoD) from leveraging capability enhancements, realizing efficiencies (e.g., eliminating redundant programs), and considering tradeoffs that can assist in funding new capabilities.

The OBRM structure enables the Joint Staff to identify issues from the assessment of tasks and objectives. Objectives are hierarchical and extend from national goals down to service programs. But because JWCA areas mix functions, objectives, capabilities, and tasks, it is difficult to link the JWCA outputs directly to strategy and resources. A common denominator was needed that would enable a crosswalk between JWCA issues and the OBRM framework. Joint operational tasks met this need. They can be identified in the JWCA areas, and they map directly into the OBRM framework. As Figure S.1 shows, joint operational tasks fit between service programs and national goals.

A first step in applying the methodology to integrating issues is establishing a baseline for the analysis. Establishing the baseline has two aspects: identifying known shortfalls and mapping joint operational tasks to each JWCA area. Knowing the shortfalls allows the staff to focus its efforts, and mapping the tasks to the JWCA areas allows the staff to aggregate issues and capabilities across areas.

Defining Constraints and Issues

The OBRM methodology enables the staff to identify issues and order them hierarchically based on the importance of the joint operational task. However, a process is also needed for assessing constraints and costs. Both are central to identifying any issues to fund efforts to correct key shortfalls. Because the Office of the Secretary of Defense (OSD) operates under a myriad of political, legislative, and fiscal constraints, we needed some criteria to identify issues that could lead to offsets. We defined four issue categories:

- **Feasible today**. This category focuses on issues that are appropriate for the Joint Staff to address now. Issues that affect the ability of the CINCs to carry out their missions fall into this category. Examples include DoD resource decisions to support readiness.

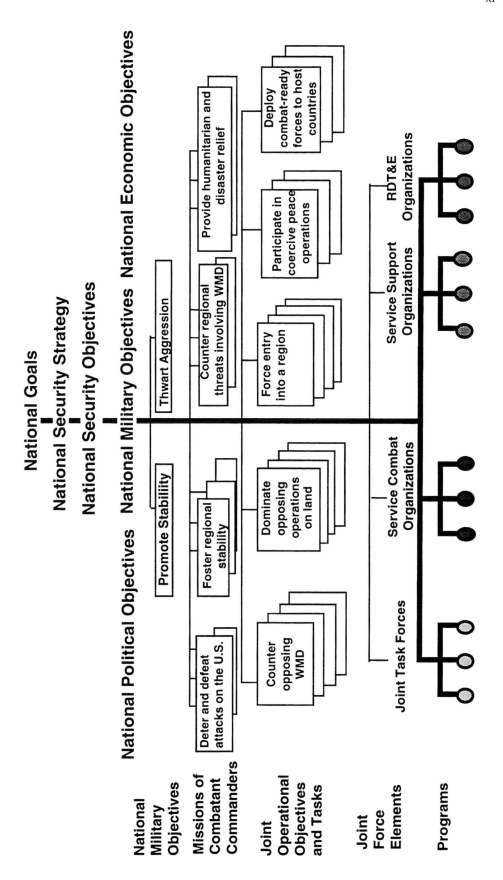

Figure S.1—The OBRM Framework

- **Feasible only if constraints change**. This category addresses issues that could lead to enhanced capabilities or efficiencies if DoD were willing to accept greater risk, e.g., relaxing the constraint to be capable of two nearly simultaneous major regional conflicts (MRCs) would enable a reduction in end strength, albeit at the cost of increased risk.

- **Issues for the Services to Resolve**. Some issues fall within the purview of the services, even though they affect joint capabilities. Organizational and infrastructure tradeoffs are appropriately determined by the services, e.g., structure of an Army division.

- **Future programs**. This category addresses issues beyond the program years. Programs now under development will affect capabilities in future years. These future programs might enable DoD to alter its current investment strategies.

The categorization process takes issues from all sources (CINCs, service program objective memorandums [POMs], etc.) and assigns them to an issue matrix, where they are sorted, grouped, and coded. Issues are then assigned to one of the four issue categories, allowing the Joint Staff to focus its efforts.

The effort then turns to defining constraints and offsets. Constraints preclude DoD from eliminating redundant or inefficient programs and can be either external or internal. Relaxing or tightening a constraint can affect allocation of resources.

Offsets are actions that can eliminate inefficiencies—unnecessary redundancies, processes that consume excessive resources, outdated programs—in the current defense program. Offsets can come from either eliminating or scaling back current or planned programs.

There are a range of offsets. Small ones exist in specific JWCA areas. Generally, these will not produce large savings, but they tend to be easier to implement. Larger ones can result from relaxing (or redefining) constraints or altering the objectives associated with the national military strategy. An example of the former would be redefining arms control limits as a ceiling rather than a floor. Relaxing this constraint might allow a unilateral reduction in the number of weapons and possible changes in the nuclear force structure. An example of the latter would be an increased reliance on nuclear deterrence, which could lead to smaller conventional force structures.

Offsets also have to be considered in light of current and future capabilities. For example, a capability that is high now and likely to remain high—e.g., deterring nuclear attack from Russia—might be a good place to seek offsets. This would also be true for one that is acceptable now and likely to improve. However, one that is poor now and likely to worsen—e.g., ability to defeat weapons of mass destruction (WMD) attacks by rogue states—might be an area in which to seek capability enhancements or focus development efforts toward more clearly articulated joint priorities.

Examples of Issues

We used the OBRM and the constraint and evaluation process to identify some illustrative issues for RAID. There were two goals. The first was to show how issues in individual JWCA areas could be identified and the types of analyses needed to assess them further. The second goal was to assist RAID in understanding how issues identified in individual JWCA areas could be aggregated into broader issues that address joint capabilities and their investment implications.

We reviewed a number of issues for potential offsets and then identified the constraints associated with each. Constraints on several issues could be revised or, in most cases, relaxed to yield efficiencies or enhanced capabilities. Neutralizing armor formations was one example. It is constrained explicitly and implicitly. The Bottom-Up Review (BUR) imposes an explicit constraint by defining the force structure necessary to carry out this mission in the MRC scenarios. An implicit constraint is that this mission is generally accepted as belonging to the Army. But a better deep-fire capability on the Army's part or assignment of more interdiction or more close air support aircraft from the air forces might reduce the need for large armored forces. Types of analyses that could lead to alternative concepts include concept-development studies with and without large armored forces.

The RAID concluded that it needed to address issues that fall into the "feasible today" category. The study team assisted RAID in identifying issues feasible today with the greatest potential for near-term offsets. We identified several, one of which was Joint Task Force (JTF) helicopter requirements. Preliminary assessment of the services' helicopter programs shows duplication and overcapacity. Relaxing some of the BUR-imposed constraints may cause the services to reduce or reorganize their current structures.

Concluding Observations

The application of the OBRM and the subsequent identification of constraints and issues provide a systematic way for RAID to assist the CJCS in making decisions about programs that affect joint capabilities in a time of reduced budgets. Duplication and overcapacity still exist within DoD programs. The JWCA process can assist the JROC in making decisions about service programs in support of joint capabilities. To assist the JWCA in its efforts, we would suggest that the formal requirements documents the program advocates presenting to the JROC, such as the Mission Needs Statements (MNS) and Operational Requirements Documents (ORD), include an analysis of the fiscal effect of the program, to include identification of potential offsets.

We also note that the concept of jointness has not been institutionalized in the DoD. The greatest challenge is insinuating the concept into service investment strategies. In pursuit of this goal, some realignment of the Joint Staff might be useful. This would include strengthening the integration function with analytic capabilities and better linking the combatant commanders and their needs in defining and supporting their demands for joint capabilities.

Acknowledgments

This report could not have been prepared without the assistance and collaboration of the J-8 RAID team. LtGen Ed Eberhart, USAF, and later RADM Frank LaCroix, USN, (Director of J-8) sponsored the work and facilitated our interactions with all elements of the Joint Staff involved in the JWCA work. CAPT Harry Ulrich, USN, provided the initial oversight and guidance and established our interaction with the various JWCA participants. CAPT Doug Crowder, USN, and LTC Frank Finelli, USA, oversaw our study efforts. They again encouraged the analysis and their personal involvement enabled the research team to gain insights on how the JWCA process could be supported through a structured and replicable analytic process.

The authors, of course, are responsible for any shortcomings in the research.

Abbreviations

ABM	Antiballistic missile
AC	Active component
ACTD	Advanced Concept Technology Demonstration
ATACMS	Army Tactical Missile System
BAT	Brilliant Anti-Tank
BPI	Boost-phase intercept
BUR	Bottom-Up Review
C4I	Command, control, communications, computers, and intelligence
CHAMPUS	Civilian Health and Medical Program for the Uniformed Services
CINC	Commander in chief
CJCS	Chairman of the Joint Chiefs of Staff
COEA	Cost and effectiveness analysis
CONOP	Concept of operation
CONUS	Continental United States
CORM	Commission of the Roles and Missions of the Armed Forces
CPA	Chairman's Program Assessment
CPR	Chairman's Program Recommendations
CS	Combat support
CSS	Combat support service
CVBG	Carrier battle group
DAWMS	Deep Attack Weapons Mix Study
DoD	Department of Defense
DPG	Defense Planning Guidance
EMD	Engineering and manufacturing development
FY	Fiscal year
FYDP	Future Years Defense Plan
ICBM	Intercontinental ballistic missile
IMET	International Military Education and Training
IPL	Integrated Priority List
ISR	Intelligence, surveillance, and reconnaissance
JAST	Joint Advanced Strike Technology
JLOTS	Joint logistics over the shore
JRB	JROC Review Board

JROC	Joint Requirements Oversight Council
JSF	Joint Strike Fighter
JTF	Joint task force
JWCA	Joint Warfighting Capabilities Assessment
LRC	Lesser regional conflict
MEADS	Medium Extended Air Defense System
MNS	Mission need statement
MOOTW	Military operations other than war
MRC	Major regional conflict
NMD	National Missile Defense
NPR	Nuclear Posture Review
OBP	Objectives-based planning
OBRM	Objectives-based resource management
ORD	Operational requirements document
OSD	Office of the Secretary of Defense
PAC3	Patriot (Advanced Capability)
PGM	Precision-guided munitions
POM	Program objective memorandum
PPBS	Planning, Programming, and Budgeting System
RAID	Requirements, Assessment, and Integration Division
RC	Reserve component
RDT&E	Research, development, test and evaluation
RISTA	Reconnaissance, intelligence, surveillance, and target acquisition
S&T	Science and technology
SEAD	Suppression of enemy air defenses
SECDEF	Secretary of Defense
SSBN	Ballistic missile submarine
TACAIR	Tactical air
TBM	Theater ballistic missile
THAAD	Theater high altitude area defense
TMD	Theater missile defense
TOE	Table of organization and equipment
UAV	Unmanned aerial vehicle
USPACOM	United States Pacific Command
USSOCOM	United States Special Operations Command
VCJCS	Vice Chief, Joint Chiefs of Staff
WMD	Weapons of mass destruction

1. Research Approach

Background

The 1986 Goldwater-Nichols legislation charged the Chairman of the Joint Chiefs of Staff (CJCS) with integrating strategic requirements and the requirements of the commanders-in-chief (CINCs) of the unified and specified commands.[1] This responsibility placed an additional analytic burden on the Joint Staff, and RAND was asked to assist in identifying an overarching architecture that would help the Joint Staff define strategic and operational issues and their associated resource implications.

This report discusses the RAND project that applied an analytic architecture to assist the Joint Staff in the implementation of the Goldwater-Nichols legislation in 1986. The Joint Warfighting Capability Assessment (JWCA) empowered the CJCS (and by default, the Joint Staff) to integrate and establish priorities for requirements of the CINCs. The chairman was directed in that legislation to provide mechanisms to ensure "that the presentation of his own advice to the President, the National Security Council, or the Secretary of Defense is not unduly delayed" by reason of the submission of the individual advice or opinion of the service chiefs. This legislation also directed the Chairman to assess the programs and budgets of the services and defense agencies and provide alternative program recommendations within existing fiscal guidance to better conform with joint priorities. One mechanism used for identifying operational shortfalls and reviewing service materiel proposals for overcoming those shortfalls is the Joint Requirements Oversight Council (JROC). By the early 1990s, the Joint Staff had increasingly become involved in providing information and advice associated with identifying operational shortfalls and meeting the goals of the overall national military strategy.

In 1993, the J-8 determined that an analytic architecture was needed for defining and articulating the strategic and operational issues and their associated resource implications to meet the growing analytic demands on the Joint Staff. RAND was asked to assist in this activity. It proposed a two-phased project. Phase 1 assessed the existing analytic processes in the Joint Staff that supported its

---

[1]Public Law 99-433, October 1, 1986.

Goldwater-Nichols responsibilities. (See Lewis, Schrader, et al., 1995.) Phase 2 proposed an overarching analytic architecture and suggested how it might be implemented.

RAND recommended an analytic architecture called Objectives-Based Resource Management (OBRM).[2] This approach accords well with military science and practical experience. Objectives-based management is used instinctively by experienced military leaders. RAND has observed, articulated, and systematized an objectives-based framework that enables the chairman to assess the requirements of the CINCs and the programmed capabilities of the services, the U.S. Special Operations Command (USSOCOM), and the defense agencies to meet them. It links national objectives to programmed resources. The framework enables the Joint Staff, in a consistent, repeatable manner, to identify and establish priorities (based on the national security strategy) for CINC requirements and to evaluate the ability of the services, USSOCOM, and the defense agencies to provide the necessary capabilities now and in the near future. The structure fosters the ability both to identify a potential problem and to analyze it systematically. The approach enhances the ability of the CJCS (with the support of the Joint Staff) to integrate joint requirements and service proposals for providing capabilities in a joint environment. The architecture is hierarchical in that it captures all perspectives—the Office of the Secretary of Defense (OSD), Joint Staff, CINCs, and the services—and provides a basis for assessing them in light of a common set of missions, objectives, and tasks. It assists in keeping competing objectives in view and assessing capabilities and risks; for example, all CINC missions and judgments about current and future capabilities can be presented in a single tableau.

In 1994 the Vice Chairman of the Joint Chiefs of Staff (VCJCS) initiated the JWCA. The JWCA is an analytic process that supports the JROC. The process focuses on specific functional areas. Initially, nine JWCA areas were identified for assessment. They have evolved to the current set of 11:

- Strike
- Land and Littoral Warfare

---

[2]The initial methodology developed at RAND was called Strategy-to-Tasks. The principal architects were Glenn A. Kent and Edward L. Warner III. Leslie Lewis, C. Robert Roll, and John Y. Schrader modified the methodology and extended it to include resource management. In 1996, RAND developed a single overarching methodological framework called Objectives-Based Planning (OBP). Chronological references include Kent (1983), Warner and Kent (1984), Kent (1989), and Kent and Simons (1991). Extensions of the original concepts to include resource issues are discussed in Lewis, Coggins, and Roll (1994); Schrader, Lewis, and Schwabe (1996); Lewis, Schrader, et al. (1995); and Schwabe, Lewis, and Schrader (unpublished draft).

- Strategic Mobility and Sustainability

- Sea, Air, & Space Superiority

- Deter/Counter Proliferation of Weapons of Mass Destruction (WMD)

- Command and Control

- Information Warfare

- Intelligence, Surveillance, and Reconnaissance

- Regional Engagement/Presence

- Joint Readiness

- Combating Terrorism.

These iterative assessments develop alternative program recommendations for the JROC. The JWCA process involves all the participants in the Department of Defense (DoD) resource identification and management decision processes. Figure 1.1 shows the current conceptual framework for the JWCA/JROC activity.

The integration of the JWCA issues was critical to the JWCA work. Integration, as borne out in the earlier RAND work for the Joint Staff, remains hierarchical and relational. Integration of elements occurs within the individual JWCA

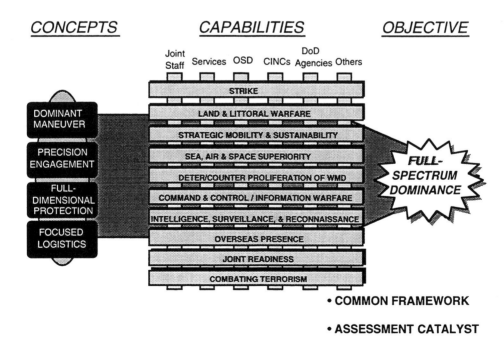

Figure 1.1—JWCA Framework

4

assessment areas (e.g., strike, land and littoral warfare) and across JWCAs[3] with a goal of linking with other processes such as the OSD summer issue review. The JWCA issues and their integration span a wide analytic area. Therefore, a unifying analytic framework supported by a family of models is critical to institutionalizing the process.

The JWCA activity provides a mechanism for implementing the RAND-recommended analytic architecture. The architecture provides a mechanism to integrate the efforts of more than one JWCA team on a particular issue. And it ensures that the JWCA activities maintain a linkage to the objectives underpinning the national military strategy. J-8 requested that RAND use the architecture to support the ongoing JWCA process and its eventual institutionalization.[4]

Research Objectives and Tasks

In carrying out the J-8 request, we defined three research objectives and two supporting tasks. For objectives, we set out to

1. Identify some gaps and overlaps in the JWCA team assessment areas and link them to the current set of issues that had been identified thus far.

2. Assist the Requirements, Assessment, and Integration Division (RAID) in identifying and locating (if available) a broad set of analytic tools to support the Joint Staff's varied JWCA areas. This objective sought to build on the RAND toolbox concept proposed and described in earlier analytic architecture work.

3. Assist RAID in the actual integration of the various JWCA efforts.

We also identified two supporting tasks. The underpinning of the analysis is the OBRM framework:

Task 1 was to assist the Joint Staff in the integration of some of the critical issues. For fiscal year (FY) 1995, two to three major issues that had emerged from the JWCA process would be selected for prototyping an integration assessment. The assessment was intended to identify areas in which other

---

[3]"JWCAs" refers to multiple JWCA panels or ribbons.

[4]Subsequent to the research done for this report, the Joint Requirements Oversight Council Review Board (JRB) was created. Two-star flag and general officers integrate issues before presentation to the JROC. The advent of the JRB has created an integration opportunity that was previously lacking. Thus the integration "problem" originally described by RAID has been to some degree ameliorated through internal refinements to the process.

issues intersect, identify critical areas of concern, and capture the inter-temporal and cost elements associated with the issues. For example, two proposed issues that might be addressed are theater missile defense (TMD) capabilities and sufficiency of anti-armor weapons. These issues support more than one element of the national military strategy and currently not only compete for resources but also involve systems in more than one service.

To gather data and insights into the nature of the debate, RAND attended selected JWCA working sessions, examined existing studies that were relevant to the JWCA integration work, and provided iterative reviews of their insights with RAID.

Task 2 sought to test and further refine the recommended architecture through the development and assessment of selected issues. The assessment would identify gaps in analysis capability, overlaps, program tradeoffs, and potential investment options.

How the Rest of this Report Is Organized

This report contains four more sections. The next section describes the process for identifying constraints and offsets. Section 3 discusses the OBRM methodology. Section 4 demonstrates how issues were identified and assessed for their constraints and offsets. Section 5 presents the conclusions and outlines next steps.

2. Defining Constraints and Issues Within the JWCA Framework

A dilemma emerged in the assessment process about what priorities should be assigned to the various issues. What issues needed to be addressed immediately, and which could be dealt with in the future? What issues, if solved, could lead to near-term cost savings? What issues could lead to long-term efficiencies? RAID realized it needed a systematic process to determine issue priorities and to identify potential offsets. This determination was critical because DoD continues to face serious program and budget shortfalls.[1]

The OBRM process enables the individual JWCA teams to identify issues within the context of the CINCs' ability to perform joint tasks, which in turn support joint objectives. OBRM enables topics to be identified, then aggregated and hierarchically ordered into issues according to the relative importance assigned to joint tasks and objectives. But there also has to be a process for assessing the constraints and costs associated with systems, systems of systems, and capabilities. One of the JWCA process's most critical activities is to identify areas in which potential spending offsets for the near, mid-, and long terms might be found and to protect areas judged critical to U.S. joint warfighting capabilities.

This section describes the criteria we used to categorize issues, defines constraints and offsets, and details the conceptual process we used to determine offsets.

Issue Criteria

The DoD must operate under today's fiscal constraints and support the national security strategy, knowing that one or both might change. In the current environment, the major potential variables (those areas in which the most resources are concentrated) are based on the Bottom-Up Review (BUR), which defined the capabilities needed to support the national military strategy. Therefore, any likely and feasible offsets only nibble at the margins of the DoD's overall defense resources. If major changes occur in national security policy then

---

[1]It is well known that the DoD has experienced a steady budget decline in real dollars. The defense budget has declined by 40 percent in constant dollars since 1987. Importantly, as the Congress begins to further evaluate entitlements, there is a real possibility that defense budgets might further decline.

major changes might become "acceptable" and a broader capabilities-based approach for reductions might become feasible.

Based on these insights, four culling criteria for issues were defined: feasible today, feasible only if constraints change, issues for the services to resolve, and issues beyond the Future Years Defense Plan (FYDP).

Feasible Today

This category focuses on issues that are appropriate for the Joint Staff to assess now. Based on the goals of the JWCA/JROC and the responsibilities assigned to the chairman by Goldwater-Nichols and the Title 10 enabling legislation, the chairman's focus should be on those issues that affect the ability of the CINCs to perform their missions with assigned joint forces. Some of the issues that are appropriate for Joint Staff assessment are the DoD program decisions for FY98–99 and beyond. By law the chairman must provide a formal assessment to the Secretary of Defense (SECDEF) of how each of the service programs addresses strategic priorities contained in the Defense Planning Guidance (DPG) and other national security directives, as well as the priorities of the combatant commanders. For the most part, these sets of issues are discrete. The activity enables the Joint Staff to make difficult decisions among deserving programs, as well as to identify current programs that are ineffective, excessively redundant, or grossly inefficient.

The evaluation of current programs also enables identification of programs that are obsolete now or will soon be based on changes in the strategic environment or the national military strategy, or whose operational value has been diminished due to new and/or improved technology or changes in joint concepts and doctrine.

Another factor in defining the feasible-today category is "can't duck" issues. These issues are so important or visible that they must be addressed today.

Feasible Only if Constraints Change

This category addresses those operational concepts and the supporting resources that are at variance with current strategy or fiscal constraints. Another consideration for issues in this category is that savings could be found if the DoD were willing to accept a higher level of risk. For instance, force structure and end strength might be reduced if the DoD relaxed the constraint of the two nearly simultaneous major regional conflicts (MRCs), or if the DoD were willing to accept greater risk concerning the U.S.'s ability to respond unilaterally to two nearly simultaneous MRCs.

Issues for Services to Resolve

Not all issues relating to the forces individual services provide need to be resolved in the joint arena. In particular, organizational and infrastructure tradeoffs are appropriately determined by the services after the demands of the joint commanders are understood. The Force XXI process leading to the redefinition of an Army division must respond to the requirements for capabilities that are developed in the JROC/JWCA activities, but the Army must then develop the concept and field the capabilities.

Future Programs Beyond the FYDP

This category addresses issues beyond the program years, positing that programs currently under development will affect future capabilities. Assuming that certain programs providing new capabilities will be operational in the outyears allows OSD to alter its current investment strategies in other programs that are viewed as less robust.

Figure 2.1 shows the recommended process. Various inputs into the issue matrix are identified. For example, the CINC Integrated Priority List (IPL) inputs are only one source of issues that are eventually associated with JWCA teams for analysis. Considering all of the issues that may be important would lead to a long and potentially unmanageable list. Without an organizing framework, issues will be treated in an arbitrary way, since there are far too many issues to address. The integrating framework is an issue matrix, which serves as a repository for information and a basis for explaining why particular issues are selected for analysis. The JWCA process must incorporate, sometimes in parallel, issues that arise in related external processes, such as the program review or the Commission on the Roles and Capabilities of the Intelligence Community. An example of elements of a matrix for issues potentially involving offsets is shown in Table 2.1. The "Can't Duck" category refers to issues that have to be considered immediately.

Defining Constraints and Offsets

The assessment then turned toward defining constraints and offsets (BUR, pp. 20–24). For this assessment, **constraints** had certain characteristics: They were

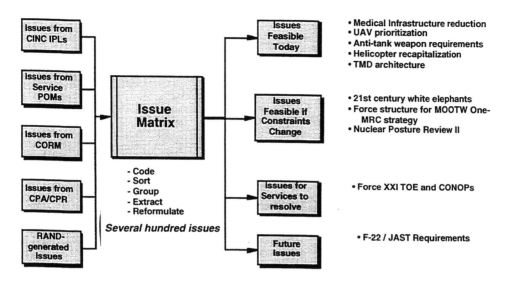

Examples

- Medical Infrastructure reduction
- UAV prioritization
- Anti-tank weapon requirements
- Helicopter recapitalization
- TMD architecture

- 21st century white elephants
- Force structure for MOOTW One-MRC strategy
- Nuclear Posture Review II

- Force XXI TOE and CONOPs

- F-22 / JAST Requirements

Figure 2.1—The Evaluation Process

Table 2.1

Issue Development Matrix

Illustrative Issues	Criteria				
	Joint Issue	Beyond current budget years	Ineffective, redundant, or inefficient	Can't duck	Requires strategy change
Medical infrastructure reduction[a]	X	X	X		
UAV program prioritization	X	X	X		
Anti-tank weapon requirements for JTF in MRC	X	X	X		
Medium lift helicopter recapitalization	X	X	X	X	?
Theater missile defense architecture	X	X	X	X	
Centralized laboratories	X	X	X		
Centralized testing and evaluation	X	X	X		
Unified command plan consolidation				X	
Restructure defense agencies[b]	X		X		

[a]Sizing to wartime requirements.
[b]Eliminate overlap with service Title 10 responsibilities.

hierarchical, in that issues were often aggregations of topics usually drawn from the JWCA/JROC process, and they were interrelated. For instance, the number of Army divisions is bounded or constrained by the national military strategy, which is formulated in response to the demands imposed on it by the national security strategy.

Constraints can be imposed externally, or they can be self-imposed. The President and Congress impose constraints on the DoD; the SECDEF, the OSD, the CJCS, the JWCA/JROC place them on the services. The DoD is currently working under the implicit assumption that Defense's share of the President's Budget will not increase. The services often impose constraints on themselves based on their interpretation of how to respond to the guidance provided them and to protect what they view as their core capabilities. The relaxation or tightening of a constraint can change how resources are identified and distributed.

Constraints need to be defined in a manner consistent with the JROC charter for identification of requirements and operational shortfalls (CJCS, 1996). The constraints are explicit in the assumptions and conclusions of the BUR strategy.

Therefore, it was assumed that strategy and force structure would be unchanged for the Program Objective Memorandum (POM) 98 planning activities.

A potential **offset** was defined as program elements that might be reduced, traded, or given new priorities to ensure the funding of a capability judged to be essential to meeting operational objectives. These recommended reductions would come from an alternative program with a negative POM increment or cost avoidance to permit funding of requirements not incorporated in the POMs. Inefficiencies were defined as unnecessary redundancies, processes that required excessive resources or that were not critical to the performance of a task, outdated investment programs, or activities that were superfluous to the support of the objectives of the national military strategy. An offset would also require no changes in the national strategy or in DoD policy.

Ranges of potential offsets were also defined. Internal offsets were generally small ones identified within a single JWCA team. A lower-priority offset could be planned or found in existing systems. Another type of offset was those activities or systems that were relatively low cost, but easy to implement within the DoD program.

The research team also concluded that a broader perspective could be applied to identify an offset. We termed these cross-cutting issues. These would include major increases in a particular joint capability that extended across JWCAs.

Cross-cutting issues required explicit examination of current and planned operational concepts. For instance, the DoD could consider reductions in its force structure if it acquired new capabilities that enabled it to perform joint tasks and accomplish objectives with fewer forces.

Two potential sources of offsets were found. The first was the elimination (or scaling back) of planned programs. These areas focused primarily on research, development, test, and evaluation (RDT&E) and procurement funds. RDT&E and procurement were areas where the military departments could get immediate savings. Offsets could also be found by developing new operational concepts or nonmateriel solutions.[2] The second source of offsets is the elimination or scaling back of existing programs. These offsets concentrate in the manpower and personnel and the operations and maintenance accounts. This source requires acceptance of near-term risk for later payoffs in capability.

Both approaches, however, suffer from an inability to enforce decisions. The Congress, OSD, and the services do not necessarily share the same views regarding what is important and should be funded. Both can also lead the services to charge the Joint Staff with suboptimization and micromanagement. The services could contend that they have more information and analytical capability to translate decisions into balanced programs.

These potential criticisms might require the chairman to employ some alternative tactics. For example, he could request the JWCAs to examine the impact of proposed alternatives on joint capabilities. He could also request in the Chairman's Program Assessment (CPA) that OSD direct the services to provide assessments of alternatives in several areas that require joint capabilities. Figure 2.2 shows how issue definition strategies might be utilized in the JWCA work. The appropriate path will depend on how aggressive the JROC wants to be in addressing shortfalls in capabilities. Because these assessments are vetted with the CINCs and other four-star officers, it is always a "work in progress" in which analysis provides interim information for the senior leadership to then temper with military judgment and experience.

Potential offsets could be found more systematically if the present constraints were relaxed or even redefined. For instance, if the arms control limits were viewed as the ceiling rather than the floor, greater reductions in the strategic

---

[2]In their FY 98-03 POM, the military departments did take substantial reductions in their RDT&E and procurement accounts as a way to hedge against reductions in their current force structure and development programs. Since the submission of the programs, DoD has attempted to rebalance RDT&E and procurement accounts because most of the services have insufficient recapitalization for the outyears.

12

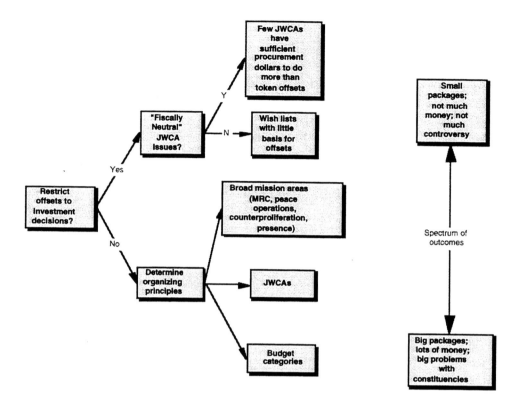

Figure 2.2—Issue Identification Strategies

nuclear stockpiles could occur. The current interpretation of the constraint is based on the concept that nuclear weaponry cannot be reduced unless START II is ratified. This interpretation precludes a capabilities-based approach in which, if we judge our nuclear stockpile to be too large, we should unilaterally reduce it. This logic would then prompt a reconsideration of the bomber-SSBN dyad.[3]

Other potential offsets could be identified by defining different concepts of operation (CONOPs) for a second MRC if the guidance did not specify a "win-win" strategy for the two near simultaneous MRCs. Similarly, if the two-MRC constraint were relaxed altogether (or replaced with a large peacetime commitment followed by an MRC), perhaps a different mix of active and reserve component forces within the Total Force Concept would be possible.

Other ways to identify potentially large offsets exist. The national military strategy could also call for more-radical alternatives. The reliance on nuclear deterrence or retaliation would provide a mechanism for cutting force structure. Another approach would be for the United States to decide that it is going to rely

---

[3]A strategic nuclear capability residing in two forces, in contrast to the Cold War "triad" structure of bombers, ICBMs, and SSBNs.

more on allied forces for a second MRC. Each country in the coalition would supply forces where they have a comparative advantage, and the United States would supply the complementary or pivotal technology capabilities. The United States, for instance, would supply space-based reconnaissance, intelligence, surveillance, and target acquisition (RISTA); strategic mobility; C⁴I; precision-guided munitions (PGMs); etc. The allies could provide infantry, close support fires, etc. Potential offsets might also be found in the medical infrastructure area, which is currently being defined for each service and its associated mission areas. However, the medical infrastructure could be sized jointly to meet only the requirements associated with military operations, while DoD outsources the remaining medical care requirements.

A shift in the national military strategy based on a need to reduce force structure would facilitate the definition of operational concepts that require many fewer military personnel. Given the high personnel costs, this may eventually be the only way to afford the desired quality of life for the force that remains. If the DoD decided that there should be new CONOPs that required fewer military personnel, it would also establish guidance that systems, platforms, and even doctrine should be designed accordingly. Another solution, if appropriate to the situation and economically advantageous, would be outsourcing many activities that are currently done within the military departments: logistics, lift, depots, etc.

The definition of the culling criteria, constraints, and offsets enabled the research team to define a process for RAID that would allow the systematic identification and examination of issues that link back to the OBRM methodology:

1. Identification of the strengths and weaknesses of existing and programmed forces in supporting the national military strategy. This step requires an assessment of current and future performance in the missions of combatant commanders and the related objectives and tasks.

2. Identification and linkage of the programs associated with accomplishing the joint missions. This analysis is based on the use of joint operational tasks and their linkage to the programs that support them (i.e., OBRM methodology).

3. Description of the operational concepts necessary for accomplishing the missions. Do they change over time? What role do force enhancements play? When? The assessment of what current programs are being supported due to current constraints. And finally, what is the potential for near- and mid-term offsets through the relaxation or tightening of an existing constraint, or the duplication of existing capability?

The assessment of costs and savings also necessitates that current and future capabilities be placed in perspective. Figure 2.3 shows our conceptual framework for how that assessment might be viewed. Importantly, capabilities need to be evaluated based on the current program years, the near term (6–10 years), and the long term (15 years and beyond).

The figure arrays current and 2010 capabilities for selected areas on two axes: assessed capability and the importance of the joint operational mission. For example, it shows that our capability to deter a Russian nuclear attack is high, both now and in 2010, but has low operational importance. Our ability to transport and sustain overwhelming force is very important, but we have a low capability to do it. However, we project significant improvement by 2010. On the other hand, our capability for defeating WMD attacks by rogue states, also operationally important, will get much worse by 2010. This sort of categorization can guide our search for offsets.

Figure 2.4 suggests how the level of capability and the importance of missions might be used to identify areas for analysis and the type analysis that may be required. The upper left quadrant, where capability is high and importance is low, is probably a good starting point. Even in the lower right quadrant, there may be potential for savings if a deficiency is being addressed with redundant forces.

Illustrative Issues

We illustrate the proposals for examining potential offset issues with two examples. The first is the Navy's arsenal ship, carrying several hundred cruise missiles, with a hull similar in some respects to that of an oil tanker. The second is a radical concept for reducing the cost of military medical care. These examples are meant to illustrate the kinds of information required and the process a JWCA team might follow; neither is the result of extensive research, analysis, or review.

The Arsenal Ship Example

The arsenal ship is a new concept the Navy is developing for a ship capable of carrying and launching several hundred multimission missiles. Its hull would be similar to that of an oil supertanker, with the capability to submerge itself partially to reduce its radar cross section. It would provide massive firepower at considerably less acquisition and operating cost than an aircraft carrier. It would

15

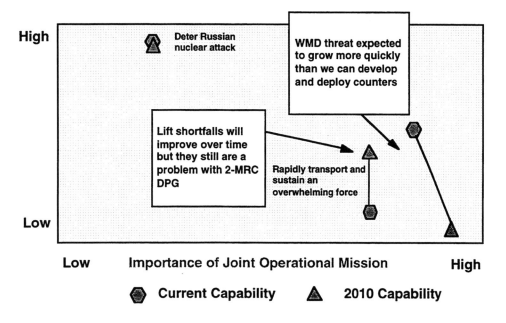

Figure 2.3—Placing Capabilities in Perspective

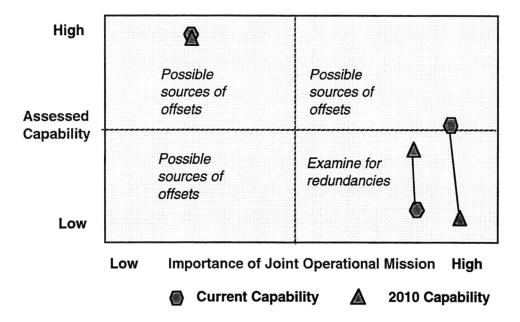

Figure 2.4—Identifying Areas for Analysis

be stationed forward for early and precise fires for long-range strike, naval shore fire support, theater ballistic missile defense, and theater air defense.

Figure 2.5 is an abbreviated illustration of a new type Mission Need Statement (MNS) for the arsenal ship, which includes recommended additions based on the OBRM framework.

Figure 2.6 expands upon the comparison of the arsenal ship with other programs that support the accomplishment of the relevant tasks. This table features the generic military operations (not theater-specific), where the rows represent joint combat-related operational tasks, as described in Section 2, and the comparison is between competing future systems and the arsenal ship, rather than contrasting current and future capabilities. What stands out in this illustrative comparison is the need to examine difficult analytic questions of sufficiency and timeliness.

In practice, each of the individual capability assessments illustrated in Figure 2.6 might be vigorously debated by advocates of competing systems. The advantage of the framework is that it requires advocates to address a full range of joint operational capabilities.

The strongest case for the arsenal ship is not necessarily its operational capabilities, which can be accomplished by other systems. Rather, its potential cost savings are significant and make the most powerful case. Inherently, it has lower acquisition costs than an aircraft carrier or a wing of aircraft, and because it has a very small crew and because of other design features, it would be much less expensive to operate. If arsenal ships were to come into the fleet, there would be offsets in terms of fewer required aircraft carriers, less of a requirement for early airlift of air and ground forces to halt an attack, and potentially enough end strength to support regional engagement and warfighting missions.

The Medical Case Example

To provide another illustration of use of an integrative framework, we now consider support objectives and tasks quite different from those of the arsenal ship example.

The report of the Commission on Roles and Missions of the Armed Forces (CORM, 1995) made the following recommendations regarding medical care in the DoD:

- Any changes in the military medical program must adhere strictly to the principle that the total DoD medical system must ensure high accessibility to quality care for all beneficiaries (including the Medicare-eligible) at no cost to the active-duty personnel, at no increased cost on average to active-duty families, and at reasonable cost to retirees and their families.

MISSION NEED STATEMENT

PURPOSE: Mission Need Statement validation for arsenal ship

SUMMARIZED THREAT/NATIONAL DEFENSE POLICY:

- **Threat to be countered:** full range of fixed, land-based targets for unmanned air strikes (TOMAHAWK); mobile armored formations (ATACMS/BAT); close support fires for amphibious operations (155MM Guns/ATACMS); high-performance aircraft and cruise missiles in flight (SM-2); tactical ballistic missiles (SM-2)

- **Projected threat environment:** advanced integrated air defense system and advanced anti-ship missile systems

REQUIRED CAPABILITIES: forward-deployed, low-cost multimission strike and defense platform for early stages of MRC

NONMATERIEL SOLUTIONS EXAMINED:

- **Change in doctrine:** increased prepositioning; enhanced coalition participation

- **Change in operational concepts:** not examined

- **Change in training/education:** not applicable

- **Change in organization (force structure):** not applicable

COMPARISON PROCESS (Need versus existing capabilities)

- **Comparison with other systems:** compared with aircraft carrier

- **Comparison with other operational concept(s):** strike operations examined using DAWMS standards; TMD operations using methodology of TMD COEA; presence impact assessed with CVBGs and rotational TACAIR deployments

FISCAL IMPACT:

- **Inherent savings:** Lower acquisition and operation costs

- **Offsets:** Reduced requirement for airlift; reduced requirement for CVBG; reduced requirement for F-22/JSF

WHAT ARE THE ISSUES: Whether the concept will work (effective, survivable); how much of JTF strike/air defense/TMD/close fires requirement can be prudently committed to arsenal ships; whether capabilities need to be duplicated on land anyway as the theater matures.

RECOMMENDATIONS: Pursue ACTD to provide proof of principle prior to pursuing offsets

Figure 2.5—Illustrative MNS for the Arsenal Ship

18

5 Combat-Related Operational Tasks Supported by Arsenal Ship		BASELINE		COMPETING SYSTEMS						
Ref. No. / Description		Current Assessment	2010 Assessment	ARSENAL SHIP	CVBG	AEGIS	F-22	JSF	ATACMS	THAAD
4	Defend U.S. against opposing attacks using WMD.	••••••	•••	X	X	X				X
5	Deter use of opposing WMD through credible threat of retaliation.	OK	•••	X	X	X		X	X	
6	Suppress and destroy opposing WMD.	••••••	•••	X	X	X		X	X	
7	Disrupt opposing command and control of WMD.	•••	•••	X	X	X		X	X	
15	Provide attack assessment	•••	OK	X	X	X	X	X		
16	Suppress and destroy opposing air defenses	OK	OK	X	X	X		X		
17	Defeat opposing attacks in friendly air	OK	OK	X	X	X	X	X	X	
18	Degrade sortie rates of opposing aircraft	OK	OK	X	X	X	X	X		
19	Destroy opposing aircraft in flight	OK	OK	X	X	X	X	X		
20	Suppress and destroy opposing ballistic missiles	••••••	•••	X	X	X		X	X	X
21	Suppress and destroy opposing cruise missiles	••••••	•••	X	X	X	X	X		
22	Deny opposing use of ports and roadsteads	OK	OK	X	X	X		X	X	
23	Destroy opposing surface combatants	OK	OK	X	X	X		X		
26	Defeat air attacks on friendly naval forces	OK	OK	X	X	X	X	X		
28	Fix and destroy opposing land forces in operational depth	OK	OK	X	X			X	X	
29	Repel opposing attacks on land	OK	OK	X	X			X	X	
31	Destroy opposing land forces in contact with friendly forces	OK	OK	X				X	X	
32	Pursue and destroy opposing forces in retreat	OK	OK	X	X			X	X	
35	Disrupt opposing communications	OK	•••	X	X	X		X	X	
36	Disrupt opposing power generation	OK	OK	X	X	X		X	X	
37	Disrupt opposing transportation	OK	OK	X	X	X		X	X	
38	Degrade opposing stocks of war-related products	OK	OK	X	X			X	X	
39	Degrade opposing output of basic industrial goods	OK	OK	X	X	X		X	X	
40	Conduct opposed amphibious landing	•••	••••••	X	X			X		
41	Conduct opposed heliborne assault	OK	•••	X	X			X	X	
42	Conduct opposed airborne assault	OK	•••	X	X			X	X	
47	Protect civilian targets from terrorist attack	•••	•••	X	X			X		X
48	Protect forces and installations from terrorist attack	•••	•••	X	X	X		X		X
49	Destroy terrorist bases and infrastructure	OK	OK	X	X	X		X	X	X
61	Suppress and destroy forces of recalcitrant parties	OK	OK	X	X	X		X	X	

NOTE: OK = Adequate; ••• = Questionable; •••••• = Inadequate.

Figure 2.6—Joint Operational Tasks Support by Arsenal Ship

- Reemphasize the primacy of medical support to military operations.

- Establish uniform procedures for sizing the department's operational medical needs.

- Increase access to private-sector medical care.

- Require users of DoD care to enroll, set a fee structure, and institute a medical allowance for active-duty families.

Our illustrative proposal for effecting substantial saving through changes in the military medical care system is as follows:

- Civilianize all military hospitals in the continental United States (CONUS) and Hawaii.

- Expand CHAMPUS to include all medical care for dependents and most medical care for active-duty and retired service personnel in CONUS and Hawaii.

- Establish arrangements with civilian and Veterans Administration hospitals for treatment of military operational casualties during periods of national emergency or under other stated provisions.[4]

- Revamp medical reservist policies such that most medical reservists, when on active duty, would serve at their local civilian or Veterans Administration hospital.[5]

- Reduce active duty medical personnel accordingly.

Figure 2.7 is an illustrative MNS for this proposal.

Figure 2.8 uses the operational tasks framework to compare the present and alternative medical policies. Preliminary review of the tasks suggests that no operational capability would be lost by adopting the proposal. Needless to say, advocates of the present system or of less drastic alternatives would challenge the assessments and would advocate requirements not presently represented in the framework. We do not regard that an a condemnation of the integrative framework but as an opportunity to consider refining and improving it.

---

[4]This would be similar to arrangements for civilian augmentation of airlift and sealift and for host-nation support.

[5]This would reduce financial and personnel hardships to medical reservists, such as were apparent in the Persian Gulf War, while providing very flexible quality medical care for casualties.

MISSION NEED STATEMENT

PURPOSE: MNS validations for alternative medical policy

SUMMARIZED THREAT/NATIONAL DEFENSE POLICY:

- **Threat to be countered:** threats leading to U.S. casualties; nonoperational medical threats to health of service personnel and dependents

- **Projected threat environment:** conventional and WMD threats

STATE REQUIRED CAPABILITIES: less costly yet comprehensive medical care

NONMATERIEL SOLUTIONS EXAMINED:

- **Change in doctrine:** this is a change in medical policy

- **Change in operational concepts:** this is a change in operational concepts

- **Change in tactics:** not applicable

- **Change in training/education:** not applicable

- **Change in organization (force structure):** this is an organizational change

COMPARISON PROCESS (Need versus existing capability):

- **Comparison with other systems:** compared with present system

- **Comparison with other operational concept(s):** compared with present system

FISCAL IMPACT:

- **Inherent savings:** substantially lower costs in peacetime and potential savings in periods of national emergency.

- **Offsets:** substantial hospital operational costs and personnel costs

WHAT ARE THE ISSUES: the concept itself and its political acceptability

RECOMMENDATION: What the proponent wants done

Figure 2.7—Illustrative MNS for Alternative Medical Policy

21

7	**Combat-Support Operational Tasks**		
	Assessment criteria: ability to perform task based on constituent force elements' capability (number; active/reserve; equipment; organization)	**BASELINE**	
Ref. No.	Description	Current Assessment	2010 Assessment
9	Maintain military-to-military contacts	OK	OK
10	Conduct combined exercises	OK	OK
11	Help combat insurgency against friendly regimes	•••	•••
13	Forward deploy maneuver forces in peacetime	OK	•••
14	Conduct naval deployments and port calls	OK	OK
15	Establish patterns of air deployment	OK	OK
17	Maintain prepositioned supplies and equipment	OK	OK
18	Conduct joint exercises	OK	OK
19	Mobilize National Guard and Reserve	OK	OK
28	Exchange liaison elements	OK	OK
35	Obtain host nation support	OK	OK
41	Establish theater-level maintenance and personnel support	OK	OK
9	**Other Operational Tasks**		
1	Provide emergency medical care	OK	OK

NOTE: OK = Adequate; ••• = Questionable; •••••• = Inadequate.

Figure 2.8—Joint Operational Tasks Supported by Medical Policies

3. Utilizing the OBRM Framework for the JWCA Integration Activity

This section describes the relationship between the JWCA and OBRM. It then goes on to describe the framework itself and how it applies to the joint operational tasks and objectives. It concludes by describing how we established a baseline for measuring defense capabilities.

JWCA and the OBRM Framework

The JWCAs were designed to focus on future joint warfighting requirements and their possible solutions. They were defined to be comprehensive in scope, to capture the totality of the DoD's warfighting activities for the near, mid- and long terms, so that when issues were identified they could be assigned to a JWCA. Their emphasis is on the development of joint capabilities, rather than the current focus on systems and platforms. The perspective is the joint operational environment. The outputs of the JWCA process were insights and recommendations that could be raised with the JROC, the CINCs, and Joint Chiefs, but the interfaces also had to address the requirements analysis process and the Planning, Programming and Budgeting System (PPBS).

The JWCA process is designed to inform fiscally constrained choices. It is designed to identify the constraints that hinder the DoD from eliminating redundancies and outmoded programs; it seeks to identify offsets as a way to assist in funding new and improved capabilities. The outputs of the process provide an input to the JROC's decisionmaking concerning the acquisition of new capabilities and the development of alternative program recommendations.

The OBRM Framework

The OBRM framework enables the Joint Staff to identify an array of issues from the assessment of tasks and objectives. The structure, however, does not establish priorities or identify fiscal constraints. The OBRM framework offers a complete set of viewpoints, both top down and bottom up, on a range of military activities that lead to operational objectives. The hierarchy, shown in Figure 3.1, includes national security objectives, national military objectives, CINC missions, joint operational objectives, and joint operational tasks.

23

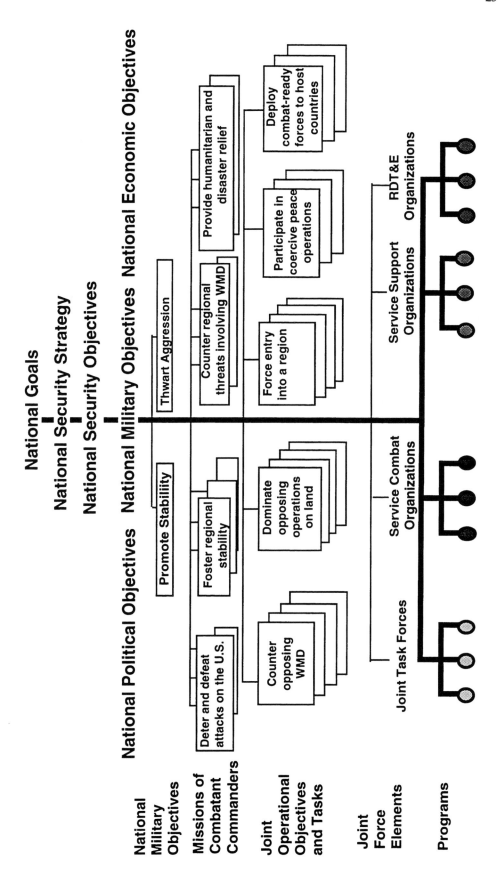

Figure 3.1—OBRM Framework

This hierarchy of objectives extends from fundamental national goals at the top, through tasks, to service programs that compete for assignment CONOPs for achieving goals, objectives, and tasks. It also implies an extensive net of horizontal relationships among objectives, among which priorities change. Changes in priorities among objectives lead to changes in the importance of the forces and programs that support achieving each objective. Seen vertically, the framework of objectives includes the following[1]:

- **Fundamental National Goals** are the country's enduring national purpose, rooted in American experience and articulated in documents of historical importance, such as the Declaration of Independence, the Constitution, and the Atlantic Charter.

- **National Security Objectives** are an administration's broad political, military, and economic objectives intended to secure the nation and to advance its interests. These change in accordance with the geopolitical environment and the priorities of the President. They are articulated in the National Security Strategy.

- **National Military Objectives** are an administration's broad military objectives as articulated *inter alia* in the national military strategy and the DPG.

- **Missions of Combatant Commanders** reflect the intent of the national command authorities communicated to combatant commanders, normally through the Joint Chiefs of Staff. Missions may be expressed in general terms, e.g., "compel Iraqi forces to leave Kuwait and restore the legitimate government," leaving commanders to discern the implied objectives. The OBRM framework presents categories of missions "Deter and defend against attacks on the United States" and "Promote regional stability." A particular mission would associate a specific CINC with a specific threat or region, e.g., U.S. Pacific Command (USPACOM) promote regional stability in Southeast Asia.

- **Joint Operational Objectives** are objectives that unified commanders must attain to accomplish their missions, e.g., "dominate opposing operations at sea and exploit sea at will." Operational objectives can be formulated generically for broad planning purposes or specifically in the context of planning scenarios and actual operations. For example, destroying 50 percent of the Iraqi ground-combat power was an operational objective during the air phase of Desert Storm.

---

[1]This discussion is taken from the common RAND taxonomy that appears in Pirnie and Gardner (1996).

- **Joint Operational Tasks** must be performed to attain operational objectives. Tasks are defined so that commanders can select the most effective and appropriate employment concept or so that force planners can devise new concepts. For example, "destroy opposing surface combatants at sea" enables analysts to assess the relative merits of using sea mines sown by aircraft, firing torpedoes from submarines, attacking with land-based aviation using Harpoon, etc. There will usually be competing concepts to perform an operational task.

The OBRM framework has a number of attributes that are consistent with the objectives of the JWCA/JROC process. It links national security objectives to programmed resources. In some instances, it can posit, based on an analysis of future missions and projected operational objectives and tasks, future capability shortfalls. The framework provides a common structure for the assessment and discussion of joint capabilities. This is particularly important given the different viewpoints among the military departments. It links force structure and equipment to capabilities. The structure also provides a framework in which various options can be generated and debated from the different viewpoints.

OBRM is also consistent with the DoD's resource decision identification and management processes. (These include both the formal acquisition management process and the PPBS.) Its focus is on fiscally constrained planning, and it links to programs and budgets. For instance, it enables option builders and decisionmakers to assess how a capability supports mission objectives and to identify the costs associated with that capability. The approach, therefore, enables decisionmakers to generate tradeoffs among competing programs within the services.

The framework also has limitations. It does not make assumptions about the relative importance among objectives. The establishment of priorities among missions and objectives is left to the analyst and ultimately to the decisionmakers. The framework must be modified and revalidated when major assumptions change.

Application of the OBRM Framework

The research team concluded early on that the formulation of the various JWCA teams[2] made it difficult to link their outputs because of the mix of functions,

---

[2]Sometimes called "ribbons," since their representation (see Figure 1.1) often looks like a set of military decorations.

objectives, capabilities, and tasks. The mixing of functions, objectives, capabilities and tasks hindered the ability of the process's participants from identifying and discussing issues from a common basis. For example, objectives are desired outcomes, so Air Superiority, Deter/Counter Proliferation of WMD, Regional Engagement, and Joint Readiness are organizational and operational objectives, while Strike and Strategic Mobility and Sustainment groupings are functions. Air Superiority is an Air Force core competency; Deter/Counter Proliferation is a national security objective.

The sponsor opposed redefining any of the JWCA teams until the process had been institutionalized. Thus, the RAND team concluded that it had to identify some building blocks common to all the JWCA ribbons. It concluded that the joint operational objectives and tasks associated with the CINC missions met this requirement. The JWCA's purpose is to identify current and future capability needs in support of joint missions; joint missions are defined by the joint operational objectives that need to be met and the tasks that need to be performed to the meet the defined operational objectives. Thus, joint operational tasks were identified as the building blocks for assessing how well the various service-provided capabilities can support achieving objectives. Figure 3.2 shows the crosswalk between the JWCA ribbons and the OBRM framework.

Many of the same tasks might have to be performed to support objectives within different mission areas. RAND, therefore, provided the individual JWCAs and RAID with a list of tasks and their association with the various ribbons. Figure 3.3 is an example of the crosswalk. It depicts a portion of the approximately 60 tasks and shows their relation to the JWCA areas.[3] A task can relate to more than one area.

The ability to assess joint operational tasks provides a way to evaluate how well operational objectives can be met now and in the near future (approximately 10 years out). The JWCA assessments are built from the consideration of the joint operational tasks. The hierarchical nature of the framework enables issues to be aggregated at the appropriate level of review and debate. For example, RAID would not concern itself with a task particular only to a single JWCA ribbon, e.g., Strike. However, a task common to two or more ribbons should emerge from RAID analysis. (Figure 3.3 shows the primary JWCA for assessing the capability to perform a task with an x and related JWCAs with a •.) The services' inability to provide sufficient capabilities to meet the operational objectives for a particular mission or across several missions (as determined by an overall

---

[3]A complete list of combat-related and combat-supporting objectives and tasks is included in the appendix.

27

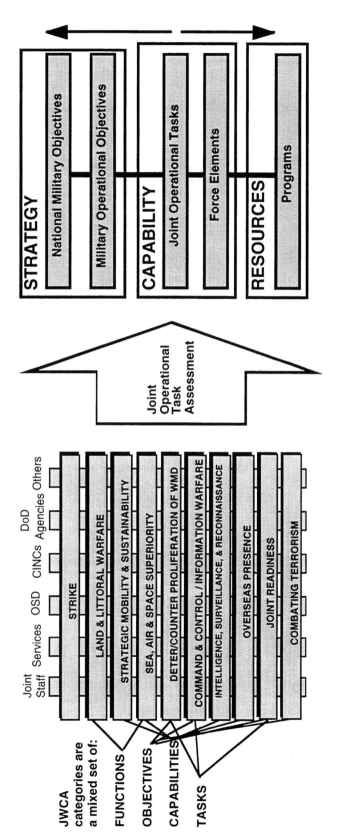

Figure 3.2 Linking the JWCA Ribbons to the Strategy and Resources

5 — Combat-Related Operational Tasks

Assessment criteria: ability to perform task based on constituent force elements' capability (number; active/reserve; equipment; organization)

Ref. No.	Description	Strike	Land & Littoral	Strat Mob & Sustain	Sea, Air, & Space Sup	Deter/ Counter Prolif	C2	IW	ISR	Regional Engagement/	Joint Readiness
14	Provide navigation and geopositioning data										
15	Provide attack assessment						x		x		
16	Suppress and destroy opposing air defenses	x	•		•			•			
17	Defeat opposing attacks in friendly air		•		x						
18	Degrade sortie rates of opposing aircraft	x						•			
19	Destroy opposing aircraft in flight		•		x						
20	Suppress and destroy opposing ballistic missiles	x	•					•			
21	Suppress and destroy opposing cruise missiles	x									
22	Deny opposing use of ports and roadsteads	x	•					•			
23	Destroy opposing surface combatants				x						
24	Destroy opposing submarines				x						
25	Lay mines and neutralize opposing mines at sea		x								
26	Defeat air attacks on friendly naval forces				x						
27	Secure sealanes for friendly use				x						
28	Fix and destroy opposing land forces in operational depth	•	x								
29	Repel opposing attacks on land	•	x								
30	Maneuver friendly forces into advantageous position		x								
31	Destroy opposing land forces in contact with friendly forces	•	x								

Figure 3.3—Associating Joint Operational Tasks with the JWCA Ribbons

assessment of the tasks associated with the operational objectives) is an issue of sufficient importance to be raised in the JROC. Figure 3.4 is an example of an assessment. It shows the status of the eight CINC missions currently and by 2010. An OK means the objective can be met; three bullets mean there is some doubt. If an objective could not be met, there are six bullets. The figures show that the objective of dealing with MRCs is assessed as adequate in both periods, whereas the ability to counter WMD remains questionable even with current programs.

Establishing a Baseline

The identification of issues began with defining a baseline ability to achieve important objectives that provided a snapshot of how the national security strategy was currently being supported and the known capability shortfalls. The RAND team concluded that the starting point should be the 1997 Defense Program, which reflected the services' programs and the OSD's assessment of how the DoD was meeting the national security strategy and congressional guidance. Many of the tasks identified in the OBRM work had already been addressed by the services and various OSD and congressional committees.

3	MISSIONS OF THE COMBATANT COMMANDERS		
Ref. No.	MISSION	Current Assessment	2010 Assessment
1	DETER AND DEFEAT ATTACKS ON THE UNITED STATES	OK	OK
2	DETER AND DEFEAT AGGRESSION AGAINST U.S. ALLIES, FRIENDS, AND GLOBAL INTERESTS	OK	•••
3	PROTECT THE LIVES OF U.S. CITIZENS IN FOREIGN LOCATIONS	OK	•••
4	UNDERWRITE AND FOSTER REGIONAL STABILITY	•••	•••
5	COUNTER REGIONAL THREATS INVOLVING WEAPONS OF MASS DESTRUCTION	•••	•••
6	DETER AND COUNTER STATE-SPONSORED AND OTHER TERRORISM.	••••••	•••
7	PROVIDE HUMANITARIAN AND DISASTER RELIEF TO NEEDY PEOPLES AT HOME AND ABROAD	OK	OK
8	COUNTER THE PRODUCTION AND TRAFFICKING OF ILLEGAL DRUGS	••••••	••••••

NOTE: OK = Adequate; ••• = Questionable; •••••• = Inadequate.

Figure 3.4—Example of How Assessments Could Be Developed

The second element in defining a credible baseline was to list all the tasks relevant to each JWCA. This approach would enable the individual JWCAs to address all the demands for capabilities. Focusing exclusively on issues could cause some relevant tasks to be overlooked. The task approach would also identify tasks that need to be assessed by two or more JWCA teams. For example, the joint operational task of delay, disrupt, destroy enemy ground forces involves the JWCA area of Strike, Land and Littoral Warfare, Strike and Strategic Mobility, Command and Control (C^2), and ISR JWCAs.

The JWCA review of the assigned tasks based on 1997 Defense Program also enabled the refinement and validation of the joint operational tasks. The review facilitated proposals for the addition or restructuring of tasks. Assembling a database subsequently led to the identification of tasks associated with an issue or vice versa (see Figure 3.5).

The process of assessing capabilities within the context of joint operational objectives and the concepts for performing the tasks provided RAID a snapshot of capabilities needed to support the CINCs now and in the outyears. The approach also enabled the individual JWCAs and RAID to determine the relative importance of individual tasks in achieving certain operational objectives.

Figure 3.6 is an example of a summary of a JWCA assessment for Strategic Mobility and sustainability. The "OK" entry indicates an adequate capability,

Existing JWCA Issues for POM-97 have been linked to Joint Operational Tasks in OBRM database

Issues Associated with a Task	Tasks Associated with an Issue
JOT 71 - Dislodge and defeat infantry in dug-in positions Issue 8 - Firepower (Gnd Maneuver) Issue 10 - Close Air Support Issue 19 Sensor-to-shooter C3I links	**Issue 1 - PGM Inventory** JOT 34 Force entry into defended areas (MRC) JOT 35 Delay, disrupt, destroy enemy ground forces JOT 36 Damage enemy LOCs to impede movement
JOT 72 - Destroy enemy artillery Issue 1 - PGM Inventory Issue 2 - JAST Issue 3 - Combat Identification (Strike) Issue 8 - Firepower (Gnd Maneuver) Issue 10 - Close Air Support Issue 19 - Sensor-to-shooter C3I links	JOT 37 Establish air superiority JOT 38 Establish maritime superiority JOT 39 Destroy high-value targets JOT 48 Attack military-related targets in enemy's rear area JOT 67 Retaliate (for WMD use) with conventional weapons JOT 72 Destroy enemy artillery JOT 77 Destroy enemy WMD in storage areas JOT 83 Support defense unique industries and technologies

Figure 3.5—Example of Linking Tasks and Program Issues

7	**Combat-Support Operational Tasks**			
	Assessment criteria: ability to perform task based on constituent force elements' capability (number; active/reserve; equipment; organization)			
Ref. No.	Description	Current Assessment	2010 Assessment	Strat Mob & Sustain
7	Provide weapons and equipment	OK	OK	P
13	Forward deploy maneuver forces in peacetime	OK	•••	P
16	Maintain prepositioned unit equipment sets	OK	OK	P
17	Maintain prepositioned supplies and equipment	OK	OK	P
20	Deploy special operations forces	OK	OK	P
21	Deploy light maneuver forces	OK	OK	P
22	Deploy heavy maneuver forces	•••	•••	P
23	Deploy air forces	OK	OK	P
24	Deploy naval forces	OK	OK	P
30	Develop seaports	OK	OK	P
31	Develop airports	OK	OK	P
32	Provide storage and maintenance facilities	OK	OK	P
33	Establish lines of communication	OK	OK	P
34	Establish forward supply bases	•••	•••	P
35	Obtain host nation support	OK	OK	P
37	Provide ammunition and munitions	•••	•••	P
38	Provide POL, rations, and other expendables	OK	OK	P
39	Provide replacement weapons and equipment	•••	•••	P
40	Provide replacement personnel	OK	OK	P
41	Establish theater-level maintenance and personnel support	OK	OK	P

NOTE: OK = Adequate; ••• = Questionable; •••••• = Inadequate.

Figure 3.6—Example of a JWCA Assessment

three dots means some shortfall,. The connection with a JWCA area is indicated by a P (primary JWCA for assessing these tasks).

The identification of operational objectives and tasks to provide the common assessment denominator within the individual JWCAs and the integration mechanism across JWCAs was the first step in the implementation of the analytic architecture recommended by RAND in its previous work on JWCA integration.

4. Examples of Issue Identification and Assessment

Several illustrative issues utilizing the OBRM and the proposed constraint and offset evaluation process were developed. The goal was twofold:

1. To identify for the individual JWCA ribbons how topics might be identified and the types of analyses needed to further assess them and

2. To assist RAID in understanding how the topics identified in the individual ribbons could be hierarchically aggregated and assessed in terms of broad issues that addressed joint capabilities and their investment implications for near, mid-, and long terms.

Issue Identification

The OBRM process developed an array of topics and issues based on the identification and aggregation of common tasks and their association with objectives. Selected issues were reviewed for potential gaps in joint capabilities or potential offsets:

- Combat identification—air to ground, air to air, and ground to ground

- Commercial technologies for C^3I systems

- Dominant battlefield knowledge architecture definition—tactical reconnaissance, CONOPs, imagery dissemination

- Ballistic missile C^4I battle management architecture

- TMD system architecture

- Mid-term JTF suppression of enemy air defenses (SEAD) requirements

- JTF helicopter requirements

- Logistics support and force sustainment (e.g., airlift, sealift, combat service/combat service support [CS/CSS], JLOTS, prepositioning, etc.)

- CONUS Infrastructure (science and technology [S&T] labs, depots, training, etc.)

- Bombers, fighters, and PGMs (How many? and what mix?)

- Interoperable sensor-to-shooter links

- Quality of life, including soldier and family housing, military pay raises, training, and promotion
- Neutralizing armor formations
- Chemical and biological defense options
- Future of air superiority
- Military options for counterproliferation
- Mine countermeasures
- Air-to-air munitions requirements
- Force structure and force readiness affordability
- Strategic nuclear attack systems
- Military health infrastructure sizing
- Requirements for military operations other than war (MOOTW)
- Unmanned Aerial Vehicle (UAV) program prioritization
- Single MRC anti-tank weapons requirements.

Constraints

The constraints associated with each of the issues were identified and evaluated. Explicit or implicit constraints defined several areas in which, if the constraints were revised (and in most instances relaxed), new-concept definition could begin that in the future might yield efficiencies and enhance joint capabilities. Some of these issues are

- Strategic nuclear attack systems
- Neutralizing armor formations
- Future air superiority
- Logistics support and force sustainment (one MRC or longer mobilization)
- Force structure and force readiness affordability
- Bombers, fighters, and PGMs (How many? and what mix?).

The development of a revised constraint issue began with the identification of the relevant constraint associated with a particular topic. For example, **the strategic nuclear attack systems issue** is shaped by the Nuclear Posture Review (NPR) policy, which mandates a floor on triad forces, a constraint imposed during the Cold War. The constraints could be altered if alternative methods of deterrence were identified. An equal capability might be provided by different force mixes.

34

The types of analyses that might yield a different concept definition are

- Policy analyses addressing the conflict between deterrence and counterproliferation goals

- Effectiveness analyses of various force packages with alternative mixes of forces with a range of targeting objectives

- Feasibility analyses of reconstitution and industrial base issues focused on emergence of peer competitors.

The **neutralizing armor formations** issue was defined by both explicit and implicit constraints. The BUR explicitly identifies the total force structure necessary to perform this function within the broad MRC scenarios.[1] An implicit constraint, accepted among some of the services, is that this is primarily an Army job. Two of the concept changes that might alter the current constraints are (1) a smaller force structure without overwhelming armored forces available in time to meet theater objectives (2) an increased Army deep-fire capability or allocation of significant close air support and interdiction sorties, which might also diminish the need for a large armored capability. The types of analyses that could lead to alternative concepts include a concept development study to investigate options with and without large U.S. armored and mechanized forces. Effectiveness analyses should focus on scenarios that vary key parameters (warning time, terrain, and prepositioning, etc.).

Explicit and implicit constraints also shape **air supremacy**. The national military strategy asserts that the United States will provide sufficient force structure to support air superiority. The Air Force views air supremacy[2] as one of its core capabilities and supports this viewpoint with a strong fighter acquisition plan as witnessed in the service's goal of developing a new strategic fighter, the F-22, and its participation in the Joint Advanced Strike Technology (JAST) program.[3]

The types of changes that might be examined in air supremacy could include alternative mixes of land-based and sea-based forces and capabilities to determine efficiencies and effectiveness. The various types of analyses that need to be done include concept-development work that investigates options with and

---

[1] Aspin (1993), p. 30.

[2] Air supremacy is emerging in Air Force planning discussions as a new capability beyond air superiority. It is captured in the OBRM combat-related operational objective "Dominate opposing operations in the air."

[3] The JAST program's goal is to create an affordable joint advanced strike warfare system by facilitating the development of fully validated and affordable operational requirements and facilitating the maturation of leveraging technology and operating concepts. The purpose is to enable the successful development and production of a next-generation strike weapon system for the Navy, Marine Corps, Air Force, and our allies.

without large numbers of F-22s and Joint Strike Fighters (JSF).[4] Effectiveness analyses that address scenarios with variations in key parameters—such as coalition support, HI/LO mixes, and time to achieve air supremacy—could be applied. Efficiency analyses that seek to develop equal capability forces at lower life-cycle costs could also prove useful.

The **logistics support and force sustainment issue** is shaped by the BUR force structure and a national military strategy that calls for maintaining a capability to fight and win two nearly simultaneous MRCs. These explicit constraints could be relaxed by redefining the national security strategy to include one MRC and some number of lesser regional conflicts (LRCs). Longer mobilization and commitment times for the second MRC are another alternative. Some of the analyses should contrast CS/CSS shortfalls from the current baseline, as defined by the BUR, with less demanding cases. Such an approach would enable analysts to identify persistent problems and deficiencies.

The **force structure and force readiness issue's** relevant constraints again were defined by the objectives of the national military strategy. The BUR defines a force structure fully capable of mobilizing to fight and win two nearly simultaneous MRCs and otherwise conduct enlargement and engagement activities. The recent DPG concludes that near-term readiness is critical to the U.S. ability to protect its overseas interests and support its allies. Therefore, in terms of resource allocation, the DoD is not willing to trade some aspects of near-term readiness for future readiness, which might necessitate reallocating current resources to invest in future technology, procurement, etc. The relaxation of the near-term readiness constraints, therefore, is the focal point for any analysis of this issue. Assessments could focus on development of campaign analyses in pairs using future forces with and without modernization to contrast with current or end-of-FYDP capabilities.

Feasible-Today Issues

The identification and review of several revised constraint issues led RAID to conclude that it needed to pursue analyses of feasible-today issues—although there was little expectation of finding significant offsets due to the current constraints—and to initiate some work in those areas where new concepts might have mid- to longer-term implications for finding efficiencies and improving effectiveness. The RAND team was asked to demonstrate how candidate feasible-today issues might be assessed.

---

[4]JSF is the product of the JAST program.

Utilizing the culling criteria (discussed previously) for defining feasible-today issues, we identified several candidate topics from the existing issue list. RAID had already identified several of the topics from its own assessments utilizing the OBRM process. Its challenge, however, was in how to determine which issues had the most potential for finding near-term offsets, based on both analytic and bureaucratic factors. Some examples of feasible-today issues follow:

- TMD system architecture
- Ballistic missile C^4I battle management architecture
- JTF helicopter requirements
- Military health infrastructure sizing
- Requirements for MOOTW
- UAV program prioritization
- Single MRC anti-tank weapon requirements.

The assessment of feasible-today issues focused primarily on competing service programs and the definition of efficient joint CONOPs based on when systems, or systems of systems, were going to become operational. Several illustrative examples were done to demonstrate how one might perform the assessments.

TMD Architecture

TMD system architecture has continuing large-scale DoD investment. The future need of the United States to protect CONUS and its allies from incoming missile attacks emerges in several critical national military objectives: MRCs, Overseas Presence, Countering WMD, Multilateral Peace Operations, and Countering terrorism. Current campaign concepts for MRCs involve the use of key hubs (airfields and seaports) for disembarking CONUS-based reinforcements early in a war. A few nuclear or chemical munitions on ballistic missiles could seriously reduce our capability to move forces to crisis areas (and our resolve to get involved in future conflicts that affect our national security). More importantly, our ability to convince our allies and friends of our resolve would be seriously undermined. Congress and the services have concluded that improvements to existing systems do not match the evolving threat and therefore have proposed a number of new systems. The new TMD systems, however, are very costly and unlikely to be available until well after the turn of the century, and an accepted, joint TMD architecture still does not exist.

The difficulty, and the opportunity for identifying possible offsets, is that there are several competing programs, which will deliver systems at different times: Patriot PAC3; Navy Area TMD and Navy Theater-Wide TMD; Theater High-Altitude Area Defense (THAAD); MEADs/Corps surface-to-air missile; Boost-Phase Interceptors (BPI).[5]

Recent congressional guidance directed the CJCS to resolve the TMD issue and link it to the National Missile Defense (NMD) concepts, given the potential commonality of the two architectures. The DoD was told to accelerate the development of a joint TMD/NMD architecture, with program selection slated for FY98.[6] Doing this requires an assessment of near-, mid-, and long-term requirements. For instance, what features are the most important to the DoD in supporting mid- and long-term warfighting needs: early initial operational capability, deployability, exportability, effectiveness, costs? How might the definition of alternative development and decision paths hedge mid- and long-term costs? Accelerating TMD development without such a game plan might be expensive given possible duplication of capabilities by the services and the potential for new technologies to overcome currently proposed systems (as was the case in the 1960s, when the United States pursued anti–ballistic missile systems). Acknowledging growing concerns over the proliferation of WMD may further undercut the two-MRC strategy. DoD needs to find money to fund such a large endeavor; this might necessitate increasing its acceptance of risk in near-term readiness and possible reductions in force structure or other modernization accounts in order to fund the selected TMD/NMD initiatives.

Helicopters

Helicopter programs formed another feasible-today issue area. The DoD currently has five ongoing helicopter development programs and is modifying numerous older helicopter types in the inventory. Programs are sponsored by different services, each arguing that its systems are critical to supporting the JTF commanders. The Army is a proponent for the UH-60 Blackhawk, AH-64D Apache Longbow, CH-47D Chinook, and RAH-66 Comanche; the Marines

---

[5]Each of these systems is in a different phase of development. The Patriot PAC3 is an upgrade to the existing Army Patriot program. The Navy has both an Area Tactical Missile Defense program and a Theater-Wide Missile Defense concept. Both programs are based on evolving the capabilities of the Aegis Weapon System to develop a defensive capability against TBMs. The concept provides for lower-tier defense with endoatmospheric intercepts. The theater-wide program couples the Aegis Combat System modification with the development of an exoatmospheric, or upper-tier, interceptor that provides a theater-wide ballistic missile defense capability using an exoatmospheric, infrared-guided kinetic kill vehicle (KKV). BPI concepts include airborne lasers and KKVs launched from aircraft or UAVs.

[6]Ballistic Missile Defense Act of 1995 (Public Law 104-106) February 1996.

support the AH-1 4BW Super Cobra, UH-1 4BN Huey, and CH-53E Sea Stallion; and the Navy, Marine Corps, and USSOCOM are proponents for the V-22 Osprey.[7] The requirements for the different programs are defined based on the tasks performed by each service during the various phases of joint missions. An MRC campaign has four phases: early entry, halting enemy advancement, building up forces, and counter offensive operations. Figure 4.1 shows hypothetical analytic results on the utilization of helicopters under current concepts of operation. It includes new procurement systems as well as existing helicopters (AH-1W Super Cobra and MH-53 Sea Dragon). It illustrates the kind of supporting analysis required for dealing with feasible-today issues.

Peace Operations impose different demands for many of the same helicopters. Areas for employment include Bosnia and Somalia. Presence operations include areas like the Korean Peninsula and Southwest Asia. Figure 4.2 shows the demand (hypothetical) for helicopters during the phases of an MRC and compares demand across mission areas—MRC, Peace Operations (using Bosnia as an example), and Presence.

This illustrative assessment shows that the greatest demand for helicopters and aircraft occurs in MRC-type tasks. This is not surprising, and availability of these craft reflects the fact that most were proposed and designed prior to 1989. The UH-60, judging from the Army's proposal, shows the most versatility in its ability to perform fairly robustly in all three missions. The AH-64 and V-22 also show a great deal of flexibility. However, we must integrate the assessment of MRC needs with the requirement for concurrent (possibly up to six) LRCs or peace support operations.

UAVs

The UAV debate is another feasible-today topic. The issue is that each of the services is proposing an array of operational concepts involving UAV programs; each argues that its programs are critical to its doctrine and support of joint warfighting capabilities. The debate concentrates on what alternatives for UAV

---

[7]The UH-60 Blackhawk is the Army's principal utility assault helicopter; the AH-64 Apache is the heavy-attack helicopter; and the RAH-66 is the Comanche light-attack reconnaissance helicopter. The V-22 Osprey Joint Advanced Tilt-Rotor Aircraft is a tilt-rotor, vertical/short takeoff and landing aircraft designed to replace or augment the CH-46E, CH-53A/D, TH-53A, MH-53J, MH-47D, MH-60G, MC-130E, HC-130, and HH-60H aircraft presently operating in support of the Navy, Marine Corps, and USSOCOM. The Navy has plans for 48 modified versions of the aircraft, with delivery scheduled for 2012. The missions include amphibious assault, land assault, raid operations, medium cargo lift, combat search and rescue, special operations force support, fleet logistics, and special warfare. The Osprey's design calls for it to be capable of carrying 24 combat-equipped Marines or a 10,000-lb. external load. The program is currently in EMD phase and has been approved for low-rate initial production. (Force 2001, A Program Guide to the U.S. Navy, edition 1995.)

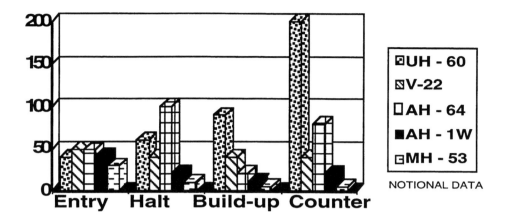

Figure 4.1—Use of Proposed Helicopters and Aircraft in MRC Phases

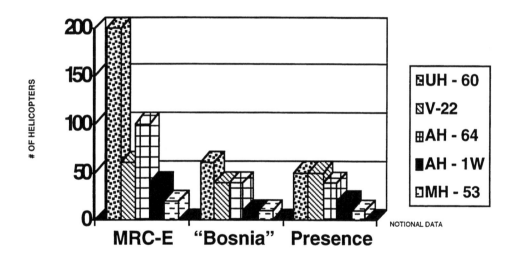

Figure 4.2—Utilization Comparison of Proposed Helicopter and Aircraft Programs
Across Mission Areas

program reduction make sense, given the current fiscal constraints. The
following possible assessment areas might help answer these questions[8]:

• Limit UAV development to provide only unique tactical capabilities (no
overlap with national systems).

---

[8]Since these possible assessment alternatives were recommended the Air Force and Army
negotiated an agreement in which the Army would retain control of all tactical UAVs, while the Air
Force would oversee the development of strategic UAVs. The agreement was reached as a way to
eliminate duplication of systems and capabilities.

- Limit development of new systems to prototypes and advanced concept technology demonstrations (ACTDs) until programmed systems provide an experience base.
- Examine new concepts (Force XXI, theater air defense, etc.) to identify what advantages are gained from UAVs and the operational and cost consequences of using alternatives. This assessment should lead to prioritization of emerging and potential capabilities.
- Identify ways to demonstrate a minimum level of UAV capability necessary to support current operations, deploy it, and evaluate the match of performance and expectations.
- Arbitrarily decide that only one UAV system will be affordable and examine areas of applicability and availability of alternatives to UAVs.

Derived Issues

The development of "revised constraints" and feasible-today issues resulted in the emergence of a new evaluation category called "derived issues." Derived issues mostly address potential functional and organizational inefficiencies that could lead to some redefinition of certain areas and possibly provide substantial cost savings.

- reassignment of responsibilities within the joint environment
- unified command plan redefinition and/or consolidation
- restructuring or elimination of some defense agencies (assigning a lead service to provide needed joint capability)
- centralization of S&T laboratories.

Regional engagement is a good example of a derived issue. During several JROC/CINC conferences, the combatant commanders repeatedly pointed out that they were increasingly being directed to perform tasks to meet objectives that were not associated with overseas presence but rather with regional engagement. They argued that regional engagement is an important element in each CINC's regional strategy but that they lack programs and direct access to resources and joint capabilities to ensure sufficient resourcing to meet specified objectives. The CINCs pointed out that the current planning objectives that support regional engagement were not sufficiently visible to allow determination of whether sufficient capabilities and resources were programmed. Regional engagement is usually described in terms of its related activities (e.g., military-to-military contacts, security assistance, nation assistance, counter-drug operations and peacetime missions). Regional engagement resources usually come to

CINCs indirectly, through non-DoD programs, such as International Military Education and Training (IMET), or from resources taken from other mission areas, such as overseas presence, associated with planned service deployments or warfighting preparation.

Overseas presence has generally been directly resourced. The presence mission has long been supported by warfighting objectives that ensure resourcing from several programs (e.g., forward bases, force structure and operating posture, and prepositioned equipment).

The RAID concluded that any proposed changes needed to be feasible within the current strategic framework. The JROC recommended that the JWCA area be redefined to give regional engagement more visibility. In October 1995, the JWCA team was renamed Regional Engagement/Presence. The CINCs subsequently argued that the current alignment still did not provide sufficient linkage to the resources needed to support regional engagement.

Subsequently, the research team recommended and RAID finally concluded that regional engagement must be defined in terms of specific objectives and tasks that support a sub–mission area. Each CINC for a regional engagement must be able to articulate the resources needed to meet the objectives and tasks. Programs currently not directly responsive to CINC inputs to forecast resource needs should be provided guidance that will affect the programming and availability of future resources.

Finally, the research team proposed that regional engagement should be identified as a separate mission area and specifically resourced as such. This required doing a "clean sheet" analysis that would result in the articulation of CINC objectives and tasks and the required capabilities to support all aspects of both the regional engagement and presence missions. The JWCA Regional Engagement/Presence team's discussions were refocused on building an understanding of the U.S. objectives in supporting these missions and assessing the ability of the service programs to permit CINCs to accomplish the necessary supporting tasks. The group needed to focus on adopting a starting set of missions, objectives, and tasks (utilizing the OBRM framework) that specifically addressed regional engagement. It then had to assess the ability of current and future capabilities to perform the objectives and tasks, resulting in the development of resource issues. The output of this on-going activity was addressed in the DPG and helped foster the development of the Joint Strategic Engagement Plan (JSEP), which will specifically capture the CINC's regional engagement priorities and the resources needed to support them.

5. Conclusions

This report has discussed how the analytic architecture defined in previous RAND work can be applied to support the aggregation of integration of JWCA issues. Regardless of whether there is a common integrative framework, any proposed changes in forces or policies with the potential for substantial cost savings will be debated vigorously. An integrative framework should not seek to suppress or minimize such debate but rather to bring it out into the open and resolve issues under commonly understood and accepted rules. The OBRM framework provides a structure that enables consistent and repeatable Joint Staff identification of issues, consideration of priorities on CINC requirements, and evaluation of the ability of the services, USSOCOM, and the defense agencies to provide the necessary joint capabilities now and in the future. The Joint Staff's goal in the JWCA work is not only to identify how joint warfighting capabilities might be enhanced but also to identify potential offsets. The savings garnered from eradicating inefficiencies, duplicative efforts, and out-of-date programs can be used to fund those capabilities deemed essential in supporting the priority joint requirements of the combatant commanders.

The OBRM framework provides the central structure for the integration of the various outputs of the JWCA process. The process is hierarchical and relational, with the common denominator being the joint tasks and their associated objectives. This framework alone, however, does not establish priorities among issues and does not determine how programs might be duplicative and inefficient, which are two goals of the JWCA process.

This approach to requirements analysis is underpinned by two supporting processes: (1) the identification of constraints and (2) defining offsets. They were applied to the array of issues generated in the JROC/JWCA reviews that, with the new procedures, could be treated iteratively. The emphasis was on balancing those issues that could provide near-term savings (offsets) against those that were the critical joint operational shortfalls.

In response to these needs, a culling process was defined. It identified four types of issues: feasible today, feasible only if constraints change, issues for the services to resolve, and future programs beyond the FYDP.

The research also proposed categories of offsets. Internal offsets were generally small ones within a single JWCA team/ribbon. A lower-priority offset could be planned or would be found in existing systems. Another type of offset included activities or systems that were relative low cost, but easy to implement within the DoD program. And finally, cross-cutting offsets were identified.

The analysis revealed that offsets could be found more systematically if the present constraints were relaxed or even redefined. The assessment also revealed that the services were taking substantial cuts in their RDT&E and procurement accounts while attempting to hold onto their current structures and equipment, hoping for their share of the defense budget to increase in the next five to ten years. The analysis also identified a reluctance to trade off near-term readiness for future readiness, citing the CPA and DPG as defining near-term readiness as one of the key DoD priorities. Since this work began, future readiness, including modernization and recapitalization, has emerged as a critical issue for the DoD.

The illustrative examples of issue assessment revealed that duplication, overcapacity, and unfocused development efforts still exist within the DoD. The preliminary assessment of the services' helicopter programs revealed that the five current programs have many duplicative features and that many of the programs provide similar capabilities in support of MRCs. The assessment of force structure and end strength revealed that, if the current constraints found in the national military strategy, the BUR, and the DPG were relaxed, the Army, the Navy, and the Air Force would have to reexamine their current structures and make the appropriate reductions.

One of the objectives of the JWCA process is to influence the JROC decision process. If this is to be the case, MNS is basically a good vehicle for presentation of a mission need by an advocate to the JROC. In 1995, the RAND study team recommended two additions to the formal requirements approval and validation process:

- more explicit vertical linkage up the OBRM chain, to identify which ends the proposed means would meet
- explicit horizontal end-to-end linkage, to identify how CINCs would use the proposed capability in new or existing operational concepts.

Here, we would propose a third addition to the MNS, an analysis of fiscal impact. The notion here is that affordability is as much a component of satisfying a requirement as anything else. We are suggesting that the normal expectation in present and foreseeable fiscal environments is that every new program "pays for itself," either because it is inherently more efficient or because it makes something else obsolete, otherwise not required, or expendable. The latter case is referred to as "offsets." This fiscal requirement would apply unless the JROC were to waive it in a specific case, for stated reasons.

Needless to say, an identified offset in a MNS becomes a loser in the competition for resources, so fairness dictates that provision be made for rebuttal by advocates of those programs that would be reduced or eliminated to pay for the new capability.

If there is the will to address fiscal responsibility early—here at the MNS stage—the issue, though difficult, is much more tractable, cost-effective, and less disruptive than if, as at present, it is deferred until fiscal realties absolutely force such decisions. DoD leadership would know how it plans to pay for each new program. Even the losers would benefit in a way, in that they would know much further in advance than now how and when they should plan to phase down.

The JWCA process is also emerging as a fiscally constrained planning and programming function. Its evolving purpose is to provide a road map to the OSD and the services for how jointness might be achieved. This evolving goal has some potential pitfalls. The JWCA process, the JWCA integration activity in particular, needs to also proactively define future joint needs rather than focus exclusively on how current constraints and offsets are defining current systems and investment strategies. The outputs of the process must be at a sufficiently high level to provide the needed road map to the OSD and the services, but at a low enough level to define specific capabilities, vulnerabilities, and their associated elements. The activity, therefore, needs to define current shortfalls in the joint capabilities, but it also must look beyond the CINC two-year planning horizon to tell the service long-range planners what capabilities will be needed beyond the FYDP.

These early insights into the JWCA process reveal that the concept of jointness has not really taken hold in the DoD. The largest challenge the CJCS and the Joint Staff face is extending "jointness" into the services' investment strategies. Doing this requires challenging the traditional service prerogatives; in some cases, programs and resources will need to be redirected. The insight suggests that the current Joint Staff activities have yet to seriously challenge and break the service "rice bowls." This insight also suggests that, as defense dollars decline and as DoD guidance begins to catch up to both the fiscal and strategic realities of the post–Cold War environment, the DoD will increasingly be forced to pare down its programs and maintain near-term and future readiness through joint capabilities. These synergistic forces might institute jointness far faster than one might expect.

This insight suggests that some realignments of the various planning and programming activities within the Joint Staff might be useful. For instance, is the Joint Staff properly organized with assigned responsibilities to provide the necessary road map? Does the Joint Staff have sufficient analytic tools to assess the future warfighting capability needs and articulate those needs in the CPA and the CPR? Is the Joint Strategic Planning System responsive to and linked to the JWCA/JROC activities, the DPG, and the overall PPBS process? Each of these pieces is essential if the Joint Staff is to provide proactively both the near- and long-term visions of future joint warfighting capabilities and develop alternative program recommendations that reflect priority needs of the combatant commanders.

Since this work was done, RAID has requested additional RAND assistance in the development of near- and long-term strategic and resource issues. This work will constitute Phase 2 of the implementation of the Joint Analytic Architecture and the institutionalization of the JWCA/JROC process.

Appendix

Operational Objectives and Tasks[1]

Counter Opposing WMD

Degrade U.S. target value for opposing WMD.

Assure U.S. ability to operate in WMD environment.

Assure survivability of U.S. nuclear weapons and their control.

Defend U.S. against opposing attacks using WMD.

Deter use of opposing WMD through credible threat of retaliation.

Suppress and destroy opposing WMD.

Disrupt opposing command and control of WMD.

Deny Opposing Operations in Space and Exploit Space at Will

Launch satellites.

Control satellites in orbit.

Suppress and disrupt opposing space operations.

Provide early warning of missile launch.

Support communications.

Provide environmental monitoring.

Provide navigation and geopositioning data.

Support attack assessment.

Dominate Opposing Operations in Air

Suppress and destroy opposing air defenses.

Defeat opposing attacks in friendly air.

Degrade sortie rates of opposing aircraft.

Destroy opposing aircraft in flight.

Suppress and destroy opposing ballistic missiles.

Suppress and destroy opposing cruise missiles.

---

[1]Based on United Nations (1993) and Boutros-Ghali (1992). Chapter references are to the United Nations Charter.

Dominate Opposing Operations at Sea and Exploit Sea at Will

Deny opposing use of ports and roadsteads.

Destroy opposing surface combatants.

Destroy opposing submarines.

Lay mines and neutralize opposing mines at sea.

Defeat air attacks on friendly naval forces.

Secure sea-lanes for friendly use.

Dominate Opposing Operations on Land and Operate at Will

Fix and destroy opposing land forces in operational depth.

Repel opposing attacks on land.

Maneuver friendly forces into advantageous position.

Destroy opposing land forces in contact with friendly forces.

Pursue and destroy opposing forces in retreat.

Evict opposing forces and secure key terrain.

Maintain rear area security.

Degrade Opposing Stocks and Infrastructure

Disrupt opposing communications.

Disrupt opposing power generation.

Disrupt opposing transportation.

Degrade opposing stocks of war-related products.

Degrade opposing output of basic industrial goods.

Force Entry into a Region

Conduct opposed amphibious landing.

Conduct opposed heliborne assault.

Conduct opposed airborne assault.

Protect Lives of U.S. Citizens Abroad

Defend U.S. citizens under attack.

Evacuate endangered U.S. citizens.

Rescue U.S. citizens held hostage.

Counter Terrorists Acting Against the U.S. and Its Allies

Interdict illegal movement of persons and weapons into U.S.

Protect civilian targets from terrorist attack.

Protect forces and installations from terrorist attack.

Destroy terrorist bases and infrastructure.

Recover hostages.

Participate in Non-Coercive Peace Operations (Chapter VI)

Observe, report, and resolve violations of agreements.

Interpose force to control a buffer zone.

Secure electoral activities.

Assist in maintaining civil order.

Assist in mine clearance.

Help to repair damaged infrastructure.

Support activities of non-governmental organizations.

Participate in Coercive Peace Operations (Chapter VII)

Secure delivery of humanitarian aid.

Control movement within and across borders.

Establish and protect safe areas for civilians.

Enforce cease-fire, disengagement, arms limitations.

Suppress and destroy forces of recalcitrant parties.

Dominate the Cognitive Environment

Formulate operational concepts and doctrine.

Collect information on friendly forces.

Acquire intelligence on opposing forces.

Develop own situational awareness.

Disrupt and distort opponent's information and intelligence.

Reduce will of opponent to fight.

Enhance Capabilities of U.S. Friends and Allies

Provide weapons and equipment.

Train friendly and allied forces.

Maintain military-to-military contacts.

Conduct combined exercises.

Help combat insurgency against friendly regimes.

Support insurrection against hostile regimes.

Maintain Peacetime Military Presence

Forward deploy maneuver forces in peacetime.

Conduct naval deployments and port calls.

Establish patterns of air deployment.

Maintain prepositioned unit equipment sets.

Maintain prepositioned supplies and equipment.

Conduct joint exercises.

Deploy Combat-Ready Forces to Host Countries

Mobilize National Guard and Reserve.

Deploy special operations forces.

Deploy light maneuver forces.

Deploy heavy maneuver forces.

Deploy air forces.

Deploy naval forces.

Establish an Effective Coalition

Negotiate combined command and control arrangements.

Provide common communications.

Establish C^3I entities.

Exchange liaison elements.

Exercise combined control arrangements.

Establish Infrastructure to Sustain Forward Deployed Forces

Develop seaports.

Develop airports.

Provide storage and maintenance facilities.

Establish lines of communication.

Establish forward supply bases.

Obtain host-nation support.

Conduct supporting civil affairs.

Sustain Forward-Deployed Forces

Provide ammunition and munitions.

Provide POL, rations, and other expendables.

Provide replacement weapons and equipment.

Provide replacement personnel.

Establish theater-level maintenance.

Provide Humanitarian and Disaster Relief at Home and Abroad

Provide emergency medical care.

Provide food and potable water.

Provide temporary shelter for homeless civilians.

Help to reconstitute civilian administration.

Counter Production and Traffic in Illegal Drugs

Produce intelligence on production and traffic in illegal drugs.

Assist states in suppressing production and traffic.

Interdict importation of illegal drugs into the U.S.

53

Bibliography

Aspin, Les, *Report on the Bottom-Up Review*, Washington, D.C.: Department of Defense, October 1993.

Boutros-Ghali, Boutros, *An Agenda for Peace*, New York: United Nations, June 1992.

Chairman of the Joint Chiefs of Staff, "The Joint Warfighting Capabilities Assessment Process," Instruction 3137.01, February 22, 1996.

Kent, Glenn A., *A Framework for Defense Planning*, Santa Monica, Calif.: RAND, R-3721-AF/OSD, 1989.

_____, *Concepts of Operations: A More Coherent Framework for Defense Planning*, Santa Monica, Calif.: RAND, N-2026-AF, 1983.

Kent, Glenn A., and William E. Simons, *A Framework for Enhancing Operational Capabilities*, Santa Monica, Calif.: RAND, R-4043-AF, 1991.

Lewis, Leslie, James A. Coggins, and C. Robert Roll, *The United States Special Operations Command Resource Management Process: An Application of the Strategy-to-Tasks Framework*, Santa Monica, Calif.: RAND, MR-445-A/SOCOM, 1994.

Lewis, Leslie, John Y. Schrader, et al., *Analytic Architecture for Joint Staff Decision Support*, Santa Monica, Calif.: RAND, MR-511-JS, 1995.

Pirnie, Bruce, and Sam B. Gardiner, *An Objectives-Based Approach to Military Campaign Analysis*, Santa Monica, Calif.: RAND, MR-656-JS, 1996.

Schrader, John Y., Leslie Lewis, and William Schwabe, *USFK Strategy-to-Task Resource Decisionmaking*, Santa Monica, Calif.: RAND, MR-654-USFK, 1996.

Schwabe, William, Leslie Lewis, and John Y. Schrader, *Analytic Architecture for Joint Staff Decision Support Activities: Final Report*, Santa Monica, Calif.: RAND, publication pending.

United Nations, Department of Public Information, *UN Peace-Keeping*, New York, August 1993.

Warner III, Edward L., and Glenn A. Kent, *A Framework for Planning the Employment of Air Power in Theater War*, Santa Monica, Calif.: RAND, N-2038-AF, 1984.

MR-872-JS

ISBN 0-8330-2518-X

51000

9 780833 025180

Developing Recovery Options for Puerto Rico's Economic and Disaster Recovery Plan

Process and Methodology

HSOAC PUERTO RICO RECOVERY TEAM

HSOAC
HOMELAND SECURITY
OPERATIONAL ANALYSIS CENTER

An FFRDC operated by the RAND Corporation under contract with DHS